The Berlin Airlift: The History and Legacy of the First Major Crisis of the Cold War

By Charles River Editors

Picture of a crowd of Berliners watching an American transport plane land in Berlin

About Charles River Editors

Charles River Editors provides superior editing and original writing services across the digital publishing industry, with the expertise to create digital content for publishers across a vast range of subject matter. In addition to providing original digital content for third party publishers, we also republish civilization's greatest literary works, bringing them to new generations of readers via ebooks.

Sign up here to receive updates about free books as we publish them, and visit Our Kindle Author Page to browse today's free promotions and our most recently published Kindle titles.

Introduction

A picture of American planes unloading supplies in Berlin during the Berlin Airlift

The Berlin Airlift

"From Stettin in the Baltic to Trieste in the Adriatic an 'Iron Curtain' has descended across the continent. Behind that line lie all the capitals of the ancient states of Central and Eastern Europe. Warsaw, Berlin, Prague, Vienna, Budapest, Belgrade, Bucharest and Sofia; all these famous cities and the populations around them lie in what I must call the Soviet sphere, and all are subject, in one form or another, not only to Soviet influence but to a very high and in some cases increasing measure of control from Moscow." – Winston Churchill, 1946

"Here in Berlin, one cannot help being aware that you are the hub around which turns the wheel of history. ... If ever there were a people who should be constantly sensitive to their destiny, the people of Berlin, East and West, should be they." - Martin Luther King, Jr.

In the wake of World War II, the European continent was devastated, and the conflict left the Soviet Union and the United States as uncontested superpowers. This ushered in over 45 years of the Cold War, and a political alignment of Western democracies against the Communist Soviet bloc that produced conflicts pitting allies on each sides fighting, even as the American and

Soviet militaries never engaged each other. Though it never got "hot" between the two superpowers, the Cold War was a tense era until the dissolution of the USSR, and nothing symbolized the split more than the division of Berlin. Berlin had been a flashpoint even before World War II ended, and the city was occupied by the different Allies even as the close of the war turned them into adversaries.

If anyone wondered whether the Cold War would dominate geopolitics, any hopes that it wouldn't were dashed by the Soviets' blockade of West Berlin in April 1948, ostensibly to protest the currency being used in West Berlin but unquestionably aiming to extend their control over Germany's capital. By cutting off all access via roads, rail, and water, the Soviets hoped to force the Allies out, and at the same time, Stalin's action would force a tense showdown that would test their mettle.

In response to the blockade, the British, Americans, Canadians, and other Allies had no choice but to either acquiesce or break the blockade by air, hoping (correctly) that the Soviets wouldn't dare shoot down planes being used strictly for civilian purposes. Over the course of the next year, over 200,000 flights were made to bring millions of tons of crucial supplies to West Berlin, with the Allies maintaining a pace of landing a plane in West Berlin every 30 seconds at the height of the Airlift.

As the success of the Berlin Airlift became clear, the Soviets realized the blockade was ineffective, and both sides were able to save face by negotiating an end to the blockade in April 1949, with the Soviets ending it officially on May 12. The Airlift would technically continue until September, but for all intents and purposes, the first crisis of the Cold War had come to an end, and most importantly, the confrontation remained "cold."

After the Soviets' blockade of West Berlin was prevented by the Berlin Airlift, the Eastern Bloc and the Western powers continued to control different sections of the city, but by the 1960s, East Germany was pushing for a solution to the problem of an enclave of freedom within its borders. West Berlin was a haven for highly-educated East Germans who wanted freedom and a better life in the West, and this "brain drain" was threatening the survival of the East German economy. In order to stop this, access to the West through West Berlin had to be cut off, so in August 1961, Soviet premier Nikita Khrushchev authorized East German leader Walter Ulbricht to begin construction of what would become known as the Berlin Wall. The wall, begun on Sunday August 13, would eventually surround the city, in spite of global condemnation, and the Berlin Wall itself would become the symbol for Communist repression in the Eastern Bloc.

The Berlin Airlift: The History and Legacy of the First Major Crisis of the Cold War chronicles the history that led to the Soviet blockade and the famous relief efforts undertaken to beat it. Along with pictures of important people, places, and events, you will learn about the Berlin Airlift like never before, in no time at all.

The Berlin Airlift: The History and Legacy of the First Major Crisis of the Cold War

About Charles River Editors

Introduction

Chapter 1: Berlin at the End of World War II

As the Soviets turned the tide against the Nazi invasion of Russia, they were able to begin advancing west toward Germany themselves, but the Soviet armies would pay dearly for the advances they made on Germany after Hitler's invasion of Russia ended in failure: "According to the Soviet Union's estimates, the Red Army's losses in the war totaled more than 11 million troops, over 100,000 aircraft, more than 300,000 artillery pieces, and 100,000 tanks and self-propelled guns".[1] Such losses, coupled with the extreme suffering that the Soviet soldiers had experienced in the years before the attack on Berlin, ensured that the thirst for revenge would be high upon arrival. Moreover, as the Soviet armies moved through Eastern Europe, they were the first to discover concentration camps and death camps, furthering their anger. The comparison of Germany's standard of living with their own was another cause of outrage, all of which encouraged the men to show no mercy: "We will take revenge…revenge for all our sufferings…It's obvious from everything we see that Hitler robbed the whole of Europe to please his Fritzies…Their shops are piled high with goods from all the shops and factories of Europe. We hate Germany and the Germans deeply. You can often see civilians lying dead in the street…But the Germans deserve the atrocities that they unleashed."[2]

Meanwhile, Germany's losses were mounting, and the Soviet armies were on the rebound, with an advantage of almost 5:1 over Germany in manpower, as well as superiority in tanks, aircraft, and artillery. Even with these major advantages, however, the race to Berlin would inflict a heavier toll on Soviet armies than they had yet seen, and with Berlin itself heavily defended by 30 mile deep defenses in multiple directions, the Soviets would eventually suffer over 100,000 lives just taking the city, along with 350,000 other casualties.

Things weren't going any better for Germany to the west either. After the successful amphibious invasion on D-Day in June 1944, the Allies began racing east toward Germany and liberating France along the way. The Allies had landed along a 50 mile stretch of French coast, and despite suffering 8,000 casualties on D-Day, over 100,000 still began the march across the western portion of the continent. By the end of August 1944, the German army in France was shattered, with 200,000 killed or wounded and a further 200,000 captured. However, Hitler reacted to the news of invasion with glee, figuring it would give the Germans a chance to destroy the Allied armies that had water to their backs. As he put it, "The news couldn't be better. We have them where we can destroy them."

While that sounds delusional in retrospect, it was Hitler's belief that by splitting the Allied march across Europe in their drive toward Germany, he could cause the collapse of the enemy armies and cut off their supply lines. Part of Hitler's confidence came as a result of underestimating American resolve, but with the Soviets racing toward Berlin from the east, this

---

[1] Evans, Richard. *The Third Reich at War.* 707.
[2] Ibid., 708.

final offensive would truly be the last gasp of the German war machine, and the month long campaign was fought over a large area of the Ardennes Forest, through France, Belgium and parts of Luxembourg. From an Allied point of view, the operations were commonly referred to as the Ardennes Offensive, while the German code phrase for the operation was Unternehmen Wacht am Rhein ("Operation Watch on the Rhine"), with the initial breakout going under the name of "Operation Mist." Today, it is best known as the Battle of the Bulge.

Regardless of the term for it, and despite how desperate the Germans were, the Battle of the Bulge was a massive attack against primarily American forces that inflicted an estimated 100,000 American casualties, the heaviest American loss in any battle of the war. However, while the German forces did succeed in bending and at some points even breaking through Allied lines (thus causing the "bulge" reflected in the moniker), the Germans ultimately failed. As Winston Churchill himself said of the battle, "This is undoubtedly the greatest American battle of the war, and will, I believe be regarded as an ever famous American victory."

The end of the Battle of the Bulge led to the historic Yalta Conference between Roosevelt, Churchill, and Stalin from January 30-February 3. It was not lost on anyone present that the Allies were pushing the Nazis back on both fronts and the war in Europe was ending. The Big Three held the conference with the intention of redrawing the post-war map, but within a few years, the Cold War divided the continent anyway. As a result, Yalta became a subject of intense controversy, and to some extent, it has remained controversial. Among the agreements, the Conference called for Germany's unconditional surrender, the split of Berlin, and German demilitarization and reparations. Stalin, Churchill and Roosevelt also discussed the status of Poland, and Russian involvement in the United Nations.

The three leaders at Yalta

By this time, Stalin had thoroughly established Soviet authority in most of Eastern Europe and made it clear that he had no intention of giving up lands his soldiers had fought and died for. The best he would offer Churchill and Roosevelt was the promise that he would allow free elections to be held, but at the same time, he made clear that the only acceptable outcome to any Polish election would be one that supported communism. One Allied negotiator would later describe Stalin's very formidable negotiating skills: "Marshal Stalin as a negotiator was the toughest proposition of all. Indeed, after something like thirty years' experience of international conferences of one kind and another, if I had to pick a team for going into a conference room, Stalin would be my first choice. Of course the man was ruthless and of course he knew his purpose. He never wasted a word. He never stormed, he was seldom even irritated."

The final question was over what to do with a conquered Germany. The British, Americans and Russians all wanted Berlin, and they knew that whoever held the most of it when the truce was signed would end up controlling the city. Thus, they spent the next several months pushing their generals further and further toward this goal. Since the Russians ultimately got there first, when the victorious Allies met in Potsdam in 1945, it remained Britain and America's task to convince Stalin to divide the country, and even the city of Berlin, between them. They ultimately accomplished this, but at a terrible cost: Russia acquired the previously liberated Austria.

With the race toward Berlin in full throttle, General Dwight D. Eisenhower's Allied armies were within 200 miles of the city, but his biggest battles now took place among his allies, as he now had to deal diplomatically with Churchill, Montgomery, and French war hero Charles de Gaulle. After crossing the Rhine River, General George Patton advised Eisenhower to make haste for Berlin, and British General Bernard Montgomery was confident that they could reach Berlin before the Soviets, but Eisenhower did not think it "worth the trouble".[3] Eisenhower's forces went on to capture 400,000 prisoners on April 1st in the Ruhr, but despite his success there, not everyone agreed with Eisenhower's decision, especially Winston Churchill. In Churchill's thinking, the decision to leave the taking of Berlin to the Soviets would leave lasting trouble on the European continent, a more pressing concern for the British than for Americans an ocean away. In tension-filled exchanges, Churchill made his position clear, but President Roosevelt was ill and had no stomach for angering the Soviets. For his part, Eisenhower saw his role as a purely military one, so he refused to "trespass" into political arenas that he was under the impression had been worked out at the Tehran and Yalta conferences. In fact, Roosevelt had promised Stalin that he could enter Berlin despite the obvious threat to postwar security for the European countries, and Eisenhower wanted to avoid being a pawn in the political maneuverings of the three leaders. As a result, his major concern was to avoid as many casualties as possible in the coming weeks of the war, and if the Russians were prepared to attack and had the better opportunity to do so, it would save lives of American soldiers who would otherwise have to fight their way in from the west.[4] Eisenhower did not share his peers' (Patton and Montgomery, specifically) concerns of "arriving victorious in Berlin on top of a tank."[5]

Eventually, Eisenhower made the fateful choice not to move the American forces toward Berlin but to "hold a firm front on the Elbe" instead. In making this decision, Eisenhower left Berlin's capture to the Soviet army, and his decisions have been the cause of much debate ever since. The Allied armies in the west would thus concentrate on encircling the Ruhr Valley, the center of Germany's industry, instead of competing with the Soviets for control of the city.

[3] World War II: A 50th Anniversary History. New York: Holt, 1989.288.
[4] Humes, James C. Eisenhower and Churchill: The Partnership that Saved the World. Crown Publishing Group, 2010.
[5] Ibid.

Eisenhower

There were many concerns about the Soviet Union reaching Berlin, and all of them were understandable. Most people, especially the Germans, expected far worse treatment from Soviet conquerors than the British or Americans, especially since Hitler's attack on the Soviet Union (Operation Barbarossa) had been so unexpected that it stunned even Stalin into temporary inaction. Hitler and the Germans were going to pay dearly for the treatment that the Russians, both civilians and soldiers, had received at the hands of the German armies. Furthermore, the fear of a Soviet strategic advantage in Europe, anchored by a Soviet-controlled Berlin, loomed over both eastern and western European nations. Lastly, even if Stalin kept his word about the division of post-war Germany, allowing him unchallenged control was viewed as dangerous to a world with a weakened Britain and a United States looking to return to the isolation the Atlantic Ocean had previously provided.

Churchill and Roosevelt had always disagreed on Stalin's real motivations and limits, and

Churchill needed to maintain strong ties to the Americans as the war came to a close. During one of the meetings between the three, Stalin suggested that once the German armies had been defeated, 50,000 soldiers should be executed by the conquering armies in vengeance for the losses Germany had inflicted on Europe. That suggestion horrified Churchill, who stormed out of the meeting, but Stalin followed to assure Churchill that all that had been said was in jest. Churchill had very little choice but to take Stalin at his word, but he was always far more cautious than Roosevelt when it came to trust in Stalin's judgment or word. In any case, he wrote a letter to Roosevelt after his exchange with Eisenhower in March in which he said, "I wish to place on record the complete confidence felt by His Majesty's government in General Eisenhower and our pleasure that our armies are serving under his command and our admiration of his great and shining quality, character, and personality".[6] In a note he added to Eisenhower's copy of the letter, he expressed it would grieve him to know he had pained Eisenhower with his comments but still suggested that "we should shake hands with the Russians as far east as possible."[7]

By April 17, when Eisenhower and Churchill met together, the fact that the Soviet army was positioned just over 30 miles from Berlin with overpowering men, artillery, and tanks convinced Churchill that the decision to allow the Soviets to lead the attack on the city was necessary. It is important to keep in perspective that Roosevelt's death just 5 days earlier likely played a role in Churchill's willingness to give in. Churchill had spent several years negotiating with both Stalin and Roosevelt, and he may have felt that time would not allow for further discussion on the matter. Eisenhower also was under pressure to end the war in Europe as soon as possible so that American forces and attention could be directed toward the fight against Japan. The campaign in Okinawa had just started and would last until June, and the extent of the carnage there made clear that Japan had no intention of surrendering anytime soon.

---

[6] Ibid.
[7] Ibid.

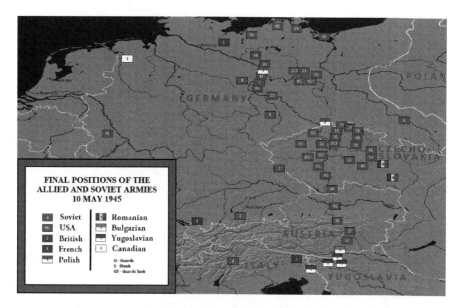

The lines at the end of World War II

The Battle of Berlin ended with an inevitable Soviet triumph, but by the time Germany officially surrendered, the Soviets had suffered over 350,000 casualties and had lost thousands of artillery batteries and armored vehicles. The Germans had suffered upwards of 100,000 dead and over 200,000 wounded, not to mention the horrors visited upon the civilian population in the wake of the battle.

With the fighting mostly coming to an end on May 2, the chain of German surrenders in the field outside of Berlin took off like dominoes. Field Marshal Wilhelm Keitel signed Germany's unconditional surrender on May 7, and news of the final surrender of the Germans was celebrated as Victory in Europe (V-E) day on May 8, 1945. Churchill delivered the following remarks to cheering crowds:

> "My dear friends, this is your hour. This is not victory of a party or of any class. It's a victory of the great British nation as a whole. We were the first, in this ancient island, to draw the sword against tyranny. After a while we were left all alone against the most tremendous military power that has been seen. We were all alone for a whole year.
>
> There we stood, alone. Did anyone want to give in? Were we down-hearted? The lights went out and the bombs came down. But every man, woman and child in the

country had no thought of quitting the struggle. London can take it. So we came
back after long months from the jaws of death, out of the mouth of hell, while all
the world wondered. When shall the reputation and faith of this generation of
English men and women fail? I say that in the long years to come not only will the
people of this island but of the world, wherever the bird of freedom chirps in human
hearts, look back to what we've done and they will say 'do not despair, do not yield
to violence and tyranny, march straightforward and die if need be-unconquered.'"

Bundesarchiv, Bild 183-R77780
Foto: o.Ang. | 8. Mai 1945

Pictures of the Germans' unconditional surrender on May 7

Of course, the announcement of surrender was met with a far different emotion among the Germans, as one Berliner remembered: "The next day, General Wilding, the commander of the German troops in Berlin, finally surrendered the entire city to the Soviet army. There was no radio or newspaper, so vans with loudspeakers drove through the streets ordering us to cease all resistance. Suddenly, the shooting and bombing stopped and the unreal silence meant that one ordeal was over for us and another was about to begin. Our nightmare had become a reality. The entire three hundred square miles of what was left of Berlin were now completely under control of the Red Army. The last days of savage house to house fighting and street battles had been a human slaughter, with no prisoners being taken on either side. These final days were hell. Our last remaining and exhausted troops, primarily children and old men, stumbled into imprisonment. We were a city in ruins; almost no house remained intact."

The controversy over Eisenhower's decision not to press for Berlin remains, but any debate over whether the Allied armies were in a position to take Berlin must acknowledge the fact that the most significant American forces were over 200 miles from Berlin in mid-April.

Nonetheless, others point to smaller American forces that were within 50 miles of the city before being told to move in the opposite direction.

The strongest critiques of Eisenhower's decisions portray him as naïve about the consequences, or as an unwitting tool of the Soviets, but his defenders call his decision "dead on".[8] Soviet casualties in taking the city rivaled those lost by the Allies at the Battle of the Bulge, and considering the earlier agreements with Stalin, General Omar Bradley believed that the Americans would have to pay "a pretty stiff price to pay for a prestige objective, especially when we've got to fall back and let the other fellow take over."[9]

Eisenhower vigorously defended himself against criticism upon his return from the war, pointing out that those who criticized his position on the issue were not the ones who would have been forced to comfort the grieving mothers of soldiers killed in an unnecessary fight to take Berlin. During his 1952 presidential campaign, he faced further criticism, and in response, he emphasized his warnings about the danger of the Soviet threat to Europe rather than discuss his decision to stay away from Berlin. Historian Stephen Ambrose saw this attempt at self-salvation by Eisenhower as wishful thinking, and that there was no evidence of Eisenhower warning against the Soviet threat to Europe during his time as general: "The truth was that he may have wished by 1952 that he had taken a hard line with the Russians in 1945, but he had not".[10]

[8] Kevin Baker, "General Discontent: Blaming Powell-And Eisenhower-For Not Having Pushed Through. (in the News)," American Heritage, November-December 2002, https://www.questia.com/read/1G1-93611493.
[9] Ibid.
[10] Ibid.

Chapter 2: A Divided City

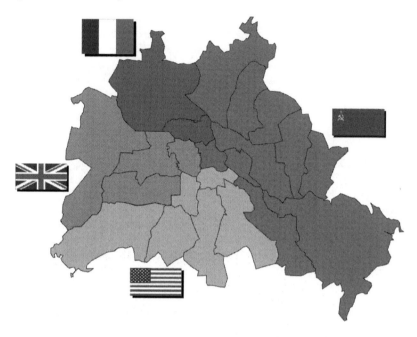

The different sections of Berlin at the end of the war

It was a famous moment commemorated as "East Meets West" when Soviet soldiers shook hands with other Allied soldiers in Germany near the end of the war, but nobody was under any illusions that they would continue to work well together after defeating their common enemy. In 1946, speaking to a war-weary world, Winston Churchill sounded what would become a famous warning about the aggression of the Soviet Union and the dangers of communism's spread while speaking to a group of college students at Westminster College in Fulton, Missouri: "I am sure you would wish me to state the facts as I see them to you, to place before you certain facts about the present position in Europe. From Stettin in the Baltic to Trieste in the Adriatic, an iron curtain has descended across the Continent. Behind that line lie all the capitals of the ancient states of Central and Eastern Europe. Warsaw, Berlin, Prague, Vienna, Budapest, Belgrade, Bucharest and Sofia, all these famous cities and the populations around them lie in what I must call the Soviet sphere, and all are subject in one form or another, not only to Soviet influence but to a very high and, in many cases, increasing measure of control from Moscow."[11]

---

[11] Churchill, Winston. "The Sinews of Peace." Westminster College. Mississippi, Fulton. 5 Mar. 1946. *The Churchill Centre.* Web. 2 Feb. 2015.

This "border" of states, the protection that Stalin claimed he needed to ensure his country's post-war security, included "Poland, Czechoslovakia, Hungary, Bulgaria, Romania, and the Soviet Occupation Zone in East Germany".[12] These areas would develop into Soviet satellite states, relying on the Soviet's for military defense, serving as the Soviet industrial plans' source for natural resources, and experiencing occasional crackdowns for showing signs of independence or unrest over the next 40 plus years.

At the same time, in the immediate aftermath of the war, the city of Berlin itself was divided into a French, British, American, and Soviet occupation zone. As on historian describes it, the division was uneven from the beginning: "[T]he victorious Allies unfurled a map and carved up the city - the houses then lining the south side of Bernauer Strasse wound up in the Soviet sector while the street itself and the sidewalk in front belonged to the French. By this cartographic fiat, some sectors of the population would find themselves economically rejuvenated by the Marshall Plan and reintroduced to bourgeois democratic society, while the rest were stuck with the Soviets.[13]

The city of Berlin was fully in Soviet hands between May and July of 1945, but they turned over the sectors they had agreed to back in 1944 to the British, Americans, and French. That said, in recognition of the last two months of the war, during which the Soviets had fought the Battle for Berlin at the cost of over 80,000 Soviet lives, the Soviets were given a much larger portion of the city than the rest of the Allies,[14] and as Germany divided into East and West along the borders of former German states, the city of Berlin ultimately fell well within East Germany's borders. In fact, Berlin was over 100 miles from the nearest point in what would become known as West Germany.

General Georgy Zhukov, the Soviet hero of the war, established the communist party in Berlin,[15] and the decisions governing Soviet action became immediately political, despite their desire to be seen (by both sides) as purely motivated by military necessity. At first, the city was governed by an "Allied Control Council" of the four powers, with each country rotating control on a monthly basis. In *City on Leave: A History of Berlin 1945-1962*, Philip Windsor explains that the council was marked far more for argument and conflict than true governance. In fact, he argues, "All the Western Powers were...for different reasons, convinced that collaboration with the Soviet Union in Germany was their essential task. The struggle for the country came upon them almost unawares, and at the outset none was capable of answering the scarcely defined Russian

[12] Rottman, 5.
[13] Mark Ehrman, "Borders and Barriers," The Virginia Quarterly Review 83, no. 2 (2007),
    https://www.questia.com/read/1P3-1256577881.
[14] Ibid., 8.
[15] Philip Windsor, City on Leave: A History of Berlin, 1945-1962 (London: Chatto & Windus, 1963), 25,
    https://www.questia.com/read/11076907.

threat. This threat would not become manifest until they were all forced to face the need of defining common economic policies and erecting a central German authority. But there was already one center in Germany where all were concerned together in a common assignation, and where the present government of the country was established. It offered a valuable, perhaps decisive, prize to Russia in the political conquest of the whole; and in the Rooseveltian terms which governed American policy, it provided the United States with the most practical test of Soviet intentions. *This was Berlin.*"[16]

Zhukov

---

[16] Ibid, 31. Emphasis added.

Chapter 3: The Best Bargain

"In the happy glow of friendship at the immediate end of the war in Europe, the free powers occupying Western Germany had apparently been content with a gentleman's agreement to the effect that there would be no interference with surface transportation— by highway, rail, and canal — into Berlin. Later a written agreement was made setting up six air corridors, each twenty miles wide, fanning out from Berlin. Three led to the east or Communist areas. ... At the time Russia seemed to have made the best bargain, for as part of the deal America set up navigational aid stations and showed the Russians how to man them. Apparently they had no knowledge whatsoever of this new science." – William H. Tunner, Lieutenant General, U.S. Air Force

Tunner

In the early years of the Cold War, the West seemed to be in retreat as the Soviet Union succeeded in testing its own nuclear weapon, setting up puppet states in eastern Europe, and assisting the Chinese communists in winning a civil war over Western backed Chinese nationalist forces. Stalin would subsequently look to press his advantage in West Berlin, setting up the first serious confrontation between East and West.

That said, Elbridge Durbrow, the United States Foreign Service officer and Counselor of Embassy in Moscow during the mid-1940s, later insisted that the events leading up to the Berlin

Blockade began while World War II was still raging. "It was another 'proof of the pudding' that the Soviets were not going to live up to the Potsdam agreements or any other agreement. We made a stupid mistake way back in 1943-44 at the European Advisory Council in London when [John] Winant was the head of our EAC delegation, in not stating in writing, in the agreements that we worked out with the British and the Soviets, that we would have assured road access, canal access, and rail access to Berlin. We did draw up the maps and set up agreed air corridors. But Winant's attitude was to the effect that 'they are not going to block us, they're our allies.' Winant was a really nice guy but very naive, to say the least. A real do-gooder with a bend-over-backwards liberal attitude about the Soviets: 'Oh, gosh, you know, let's not be too harsh because that will cause them to go the other way. They are not going to do something like that.' I guess that's why the poor fellow shot himself; he realized that all his dreams had not come true or had gone completely sour. We did not stipulate assured ground access to Berlin in the EAC agreements of 1943-44."

Even as the Soviets expanded their influence, Stalin and his advisors were becoming increasingly paranoid about Western interference in their affairs. They suspected, and rightly so, that the Americans and their European allies wanted to drive them from the city, while they wanted to be free of those who opposed their ideas and gain full control of the conquered city. And as everyone knew, the Soviets were more than willing to murder and starve anyone who stood in their way.

Tensions mounted in the Allied Kommandantura, the ruling body of occupied Germany, and slowly, the Soviets began to crackdown on transport into and out of their part of Berlin. By June 1948, the crackdown had become serious enough that President Harry Truman told the graduating class of the University of California, "The division has not been between the United States and the Soviet Union, but between the Soviet Union and the free nations of the world. The United States is strongly devoted to the principle of discussion and negotiation in settling international differences. We do not believe in settling differences by force. There are certain types of disputes in international affairs which can and must be settled by negotiation and agreement. But there are others which are not susceptible to negotiation. There is nothing to negotiate when one nation disregards the principles of international conduct to which all the members of the United Nations have subscribed. There is nothing to negotiate when one nation habitually uses coercion and open aggression in international affairs. What the world needs in order to regain a sense of security is an end to Soviet obstruction and aggression."

Truman

That same month, the Western Allies issued a new currency for the city. Called the Deutschmark, it was designed to stabilize the economy and drive down the black market. General William H. Draper, Jr., then Under Secretary of the Army, explained, "We knew for some weeks that this situation was rising, that trouble was brewing. We were having constant arguments in the quadripartite council in Berlin. I was in Washington. I stayed up several nights all night long as we followed these negotiations, partly because of the difference in time. Instructions had to be given almost momentarily, sometimes by scramble telephone or by cable. And we watched the rising emotion and the rising level of argument with the realization that we were perhaps moving even toward war with Russia. When finally the revaluation of the currency, of the German mark, was decided on by the three powers in order to put the economy back on a money basis rather than a ration basis -- because up to that time, people had pockets full of paper money but unless they had a ration ticket to buy an overcoat or to get food (unless it was through the black market), they had no way to buy. The purpose was to squeeze the juice out of the overvalued currency and put it down to its real value. The result turned out later to be the right thing to have done. The goods came out of hiding and the economy began to get back on its feet."

Draper, Jr.

When the Soviets learned about this, they left the Kommandantura and announced that they would also issue a new currency to be used not just in their zone but throughout Berlin. By that time, however, the Allies were one step ahead of them and had their currency in place by June 23. Furious, the Soviets ordered the borders between their quarter and the rest of Berlin closed. William H. Tunner, a Lieutenant General in the U.S. Air Force who was involved in the airlift, later discussed the immediate impact the Soviets' new blockade had on West Berliners: "News of the blockade, three years after the end of World War II, had come as much of a surprise to me as to most other American citizens. I, too, had been trying to begin a normal life after the war, but in my case it wasn't possible. ... Early in 1948 the whole of the Air Transport Command was combined with a few squadrons of the Naval Air Transport Service to become the Military Air Transport Service. It was to have been a great combining of competing service activities, just what the public wanted...The Germans residing in the American, British, and French zones of the city making up West Berlin were terrified. They remembered all too well when the Russian troops poured into the city to rape, loot, and murder. It was obvious that the Soviets intended to drive the Western powers from Berlin and engulf the whole city. By June 24 the blockade was complete. Reason given for the termination of rail service was 'technical difficulties.' Bridges were declared unsafe, and a one hundred-yard stretch of the railroad was torn up. No foodstuffs, or any other supplies, could be brought into the three western zones of the city by surface transportation. The Soviets announced that all food brought into Berlin from East Germany would be distributed in the East Sector only; it would be necessary for residents of West Berlin to register there in order to get it. Few did so. When the blockade began, food stockpiles were sufficient for thirty days. Mayor-elect Ernst Reuter, addressing a mass meeting of over eighty thousand Berliners on the afternoon of June 24, called for a united defiance of Communism and was answered by a roar of approval."

Bundesarchiv, Bild 183-S85097
Foto: Heilig, Walter | 11. Mai 1949

Bundesarchiv, Bild 183-S85101
Foto: Heilig, Walter | 11. Mai 1949

Pictures of the Soviets setting up the blockade

Etza Reuter, whose father Ernest was then the mayor of Berlin, described the political conditions in Berlin at the time, and the general sense of powerlessness that his father had: "That atmosphere was a very tense atmosphere again, full of possibilities that the Russians would try to enforce their power in that part of the country and in the city of Berlin, of course. That maybe the family, again, would have to flee from dictatorship. That the take-over of the city would probably…even result in a third world war. Nobody could tell at that point of time, what really the end of the story would be. So we, as historical observers know what the outcome was. But people active at that time did not. So it was an atmosphere of nervosity, but also of an atmosphere of self-reliance because at least at that time my father and his political friends, and also the other members of the city government, were deeply convinced that the population - the Berlin population - would be ready to stand. Even to very, very strong and powerful measures of the Soviets. But the atmosphere was tense enough, yes. … The final decisions at that time, of course, basically being taken in Washington. And also, of course, in London and Paris, but basically in Washington. And of course my father was quite well aware that inside the US administration there were at least two different basic opinions on what to do, what the reaction should be, what the degree of reacting to the Soviet challenge should be."

Reuter

For the average citizens who found themselves on the wrong side of divided Berlin, the main concern was not the geopolitical ramifications of the situation but basic survival. Mercedes Wild was just a child at the time, but she remembered, "My mother was very upset. She said: now we'll have nothing to eat. We've been blockaded. I didn't know what 'blockade' meant. But they used that word, right from the start. And I'll never forget my grandmother's words: 'Just as long as we don't end up Russian.'"

On the other side of the lines that were quickly being drawn, the Allies wrestled with what to do. One obvious option was to withdraw and leave all of Berlin to the Soviets, and after nearly 6 long years of war, it seemed to many that it simply not worth getting involved in another potential fight. As one Berlin resident named Gerhard Bürger put it, "It was like an eclipse of the sun. Nobody knew what was going on. We asked the Americans, what's up? They said, 'we've packed our bags.'" And so it seemed, for while there were still about 20,000 troops on the Allied side of the blockade, this was not nearly enough to fight off the entire Soviet Army.

At the same time, if the blockade stayed in place, thousands of people would begin to die of starvation and exposure within the next two months. This was unacceptable in the eyes of Truman, and he figured it would be in the eyes of the American people, so he turned to his best advisors in search of a solution. One of them, General Lucius Clay, the United States Military Governor in Germany, had one. According to Edloe Donnan, who knew Clay while he was in Germany, Clay "was a very, very tough person. But he had a brilliant mind. And, he was a great detail man, he wanted to know everything. He didn't want anybody to try to second guess him on anything. He was tough. But everybody respected him for his ability because he worked 10 to 12 hours a day, 7 days a week."

Clay

True to his reputation, Clay had a tough idea: send troops marching on the road to Berlin, thus forcing a showdown. However, Truman rejected this plan. Tunner observed, "The first reaction of General Lucius D. Clay, United States Military Governor, was to propose putting an American armored column on the road to Berlin immediately. In Washington the Joint Chiefs of Staff considered this proposition and approved it with the proviso that the armored column would not attempt to shoot its way through; if the Russians stood fast, the convoy would withdraw. It was well known that the Western powers had only a few weakened divisions in Germany; the Russians had thirty full-strength divisions in their zone, backed up by many more in Poland and Czechoslovakia. Clay refused to proceed under those conditions. 'I'll never order troops of mine to run from the Reds without a fight,' he said."

Since that wasn't an option, others had to be found, and Elbridge Durbrow later discussed the extensive talks and negotiations that went into deciding what action to take: "A lot of people said, 'Let's let an armored division, go down the autobahn and bring the supplies in.' Bedell Smith, oddly enough, was dead against doing that. ... Bedell argued back and forth by telegrams with Clay on this thing. He said, 'Now the Soviets would make us look like monkeys. They would see to it that all the culverts all of a sudden 'collapsed' -- little bits of bridges would be 'washed out.' You couldn't get over the roads unless we used treaded trucks. Yes, they will make you look like monkeys.'"

Smith

At this point, an obvious, albeit, proposal was discussed; while the Soviets could easily block the roads, rails, and canals, they could not block the skies. Somewhat fittingly, Draper, Jr. recalled planning the Allied response while flying over the Atlantic. "On the way over we planned the airlift. General [Albert] Wedemeyer had had charge of the airlift over the hump in India earlier during the war, so he had a pretty good idea of what the different types of planes would carry in the way of tonnage, and how often a plane could land at an airport, through actual experience. I had negotiated in Berlin with the Russians for the feeding of Berlin some years before, for the British and American sectors, and later these included the French, so I knew the tonnage of food necessary on a ration level to feed the two and a half million people in those sectors of the city. We both knew the number of planes we had in Europe. They were DC-3s, the old DC-3, or C-47 in Army parlance, the workhorse of the war. We had about a hundred of them. They would each carry about two and a half tons of food on a trip, and you had to allow about a two minute leeway for a landing during the day, and a little more at night, quite a little more at night. So we figured whether or not was a physical possibility to feed that many people with that many planes, if we had the pilots and the airfields, and all the necessary organization was set up. We came to the conclusion that it was a possibility but not a sure thing, and that it was worth trying."

Wedemeyer

Obviously, America could not accomplish the airlift on its own, and Draper knew that other European countries would have to help, but they were still trying to recover from the war and were also short on everything. He continued, "So when we got to London…and…went…to see

Bevin, who was the Foreign Minister still, in London. We told him our plan, and he said, 'All right, we'll add twenty-five planes.' All they had that were available. 'We're all for it,' he said. 'You never can make it work; you never can feed two or three million people from the air, but we'll make a great psychological impression. The Russians are trying to starve the Germans and we're trying to feed them. I'd suggest you take milk powder and chocolate and things of that kind for the women and children and make it as much of a psychological show as you can, and it will give us a little more time for negotiations. But it will never succeed.' ... Then we went on to Paris. We didn't know what the French government's attitude would be. We found them just as much for it as we were, or as were the British. They had no planes to offer, but they would be backing it, and they had an airfield in Berlin and that would be at our disposal. ... In the meantime, I had talked to General Clay on the scramble telephone and had given him our figures and our conclusions. He had been doing similar figuring and he'd come to the same conclusion, that it was worth trying. So we got to Berlin the next day, and General Clay called in his people and we exchanged thoughts and ideas and figures and he called in his Air Force commander and the airlift started a day or two later…There was no recourse but to take to the air. To supply American forces in Berlin by air would not present too much of a problem; many items were already being flown in from bases in the American Zone. But what about the civilian population? Could an airlift provide the 2,250,000 people of West Berlin with sufficient supplies? Suppose the blockade extended into the winter, when the population would be subjected to the even greater privations of cold and darkness? At this point, even to think of supplying a city by air alone was daring. It had never been done before. Although we who had operated the Hump Airlift considered that we had proved the capability of airlifting anything anywhere, there were many in the government and in the military, too, who had not heard the word. ... It was finally decided, there in that frenzied session the evening of June 24, that food could probably be brought in by air. But even at that stage General Clay and his staff could see that the commodity which would place the greatest strain on an airlift would be coal — coal to furnish light and power to keep the city going and, in the long winter to come, to provide some warmth."

For his part, Clay had serious reservations about the chances of the airlift working, and he later mentioned sharing his concerns with Truman during a meeting: "My first direct contact with him was when I came back to talk about the airlift and to secure his approval on it (which he gave me). ... On my second trip, I came back because I knew that if we could get some more DC-4s, the airlift would be successful. We'd had some, but not enough. We had about 40 DC-4s left, and the chief of their forces did not want to give them to me on the basis that he would have all of his forces committed. If a war came they would be destroyed and we'd be without transport. That was all brought up at a meeting of the National Security Council over which the President presided. I made an impassioned plea (at least I thought it was impassioned), supported by Mr. Murphy, but the Joint Chiefs and everybody else were opposed. Without these airplanes I don't think the airlift could have made it, and I was obviously quite depressed."

That might have been the end of the matter had Truman not been so determined to support

West Berlin and keep the Soviets at bay. Clay explained, "As the meeting ended and as we were walking out of the door the President said to me and Ken Royall, the Secretary of the Army, 'Come on into my office.' We went into his office and he said something like this, 'You're not feeling very happy about this are you, Clay?' I said, 'No, Sir, I'm not. I think that this is going to make our efforts a failure, and I'm afraid what will happen to Europe if it does fail.' He said, 'Don't you worry, you're going to get your airplanes.' I said, 'Mr. Truman, as I leave here there are going to be reporters out there asking me what's happened. May I tell them that?' He said, 'You may.' I went right out and told the newspapers we were getting these airplanes, and we got them. From then on out there was no longer any problem, to my part, of the airlift being a success."

Clay concluded his remarks with an astute observation: "Truman realized that the Berlin crisis was a political war, not a physical military war. I am not being critical of the Joint Chiefs of Staff, because I think they visualized it as a military operation; in that sense of the word they were correct. Truman's a man of great courage and he didn't hesitate to make his own decisions."

Chapter 4: A Very Big Operation

"In all of Europe the Air Force had just exactly 102 C-47's, of less than three tons capacity, and two C-54's, of ten tons capacity. The British also had a few C-47's — which they called Dakotas — on hand. This was the fleet which was going to supply the city of Berlin. The Airlift ran more or less by itself until Brigadier General Joseph Smith, commander of the military post at Wiesbaden, was tapped for the job in addition to his other duties. The news was broken to him at lunch on June 27. In the first forty-eight hours, eighty tons of flour, milk, and medicine were flown into Berlin. By July 7 the one thousand-ton mark was reached. This included the first shipment of coal, packed in GI duffel bags. During these first few days an attempt was made to glamorize the airlift with a fancy name. "Hell's fire," Smith said, "we're hauling grub. Call it Operation Vittles." The British sneaked in a pun on then: title: Operation Plane Fare. ... Clay, at the beginning, estimated seven hundred tons a day as the maximum to be expected from even a "very big operation." No one in authority at the time expected the Airlift would last very long. It was President Truman's opinion that the Airlift would serve only to stretch out the stockpile of rations in Berlin and thus gain time for negotiations." – William H. Tunner

Picture of a supply plane unloading flour

Once it was decided to airlift supplies to Berlin, the next question that had to be answered was how much was needed, and to answer this, America turned to its Allied expert on rationing: Great Britain. The British reported that, in their experience, the average adult needed around 1,700 calories a day to survive, which would require delivering about 1,500 tons of food to the area each day.

Of course, there were other factors that had to be taken into account. For example, the food had to be cooked, and people had to have lights and power to continue functioning. It was concluded that this would require another 2,500 tons of coal and gasoline per day. Put together, this meant the Allies would have to fly 4,000 tons of supplies into Berlin each day to keep its citizens alive and functioning, and given that each C-47 could carry about three tons per trip, the air forces would have to fly in excess of 1,300 missions a day. Thus, that's what they did, beginning on June 26, 1948.

Bundesarchiv, Bild 146-1985-064-02A
Foto: o.Ang. | 28. Juli 1948

Bundesarchiv, Bild 146-1985-064-04A
Foto: o.Ang. | 28. Juli 1948

Bundesarchiv, Bild 146-1985-064-06A
Foto: o.Ang. | 26. Juli 1948

Pictures of supplies being handled during the airlift

Mayor Reuter, himself a former Communist, was extremely enthusiastic about the airlift. William Heimlich, then the head of U.S. intelligence in Berlin, noted, "Reuter had emerged because Reuter was a unique person. He had been a Communist after the First World War; he was a close associate of Lenin, he knew Stalin personally. He had returned from the Soviet Union in 1918 to form the KPD, the Communist Party Germany, and then bolted from the Kommunistischs, defected and became a democrat, a Social Democrat, a member of the Reichstag and in due course had to flee Germany, went to Turkey, became, I believe, a Professor at Ankara and with the help of the British Labour government returned to Germany in 1945, about the same time Willy Brandt did. There was such apathy, such disinterest in all things political - such fear of things political, that I doubt very much they would have gotten organised as quickly as they did. Doctor Otto Suer of the SPD, who was very powerful in Berlin, and very influential, still did not have the charisma that was necessary to cause the people to take new renewed interest the way Reuter did." Upon learning of the planned airlift, Reuter organized a rally to encourage his people to persevere, telling them, "Berlin will not be next on the Soviet list! We'll used every means at our disposal to resist the forces of oppression who want to make us slaves of a single party system!" When Clay tried to warn him that the plan might not work, Reuter insisted, "You take care of the airlift, I'll take care of the Berliners."

On June 30, Truman's Secretary of State, former Army Chief of Staff George C. Marshall (who had helped rebuild Europe with the Marshall Plan named after him), told the press, "We are in Berlin as a result of agreements between the Governments on the areas of occupation in Germany, and we intend to stay. The Soviet attempt to blockade the German civilian population of Berlin raises basic questions of serious import with which we expect to deal promptly. Meanwhile, maximum use of air transport will be made to supply the civilian population. It has been found, after study, that the tonnage of foodstuffs and supplies which can be lifted by air is greater than had at first been assumed."

Marshall

With so many pilots needed, the call went out around the world for help. Air Force pilot Gail Halvorsen was comfortably stationed in Mobile, Alabama when he was told to ship out again to Europe. He later admitted, "So I had a four-door, brand new Chevrolet car. This was just before the Airlift started. This was in early '48. So then I was doing big-time. I called a girl for a date. I'd take her in the car. She said 'Wow, this is pretty neat. New car.' Very few new cars then. That was the car when I got the telephone call about the Airlift, I didn't have time to do anything with it. I just drove it under the pine trees on the air base at Brookley, took the keys, and left the car there. I never saw it again. … My feelings for the Germans were not very good. I mean, Hitler started this thing, he caused all this chaos, he caused one of my buddies to get shot down, I don't know where he is yet. They never did find his body. So I didn't have good feelings about the Germans."

However, Halvorsen soon discovered that flying supplies was very different than dropping bombs or moving troops, and it had a distinct effect on his relationship with the German people. He later said of his first delivery, made to the Tempelhof Airport, "I had 20,000 pounds of flour on the airplane, 20,000 pounds of flour. Landed at Tempelhof, and I wondered what these supermen were going to look like; you know, all this propaganda built up through the years, coming face to face with them. The back doors of my airplane opened and about eight Germans came piling in to the back of the airplane. And that first man, the first three or four came up, straight up to me and put out their hand, and their eyes were moist, and I couldn't understand what they said but I could understand their feeling immediately. They looked at the flour and looked back at me like I was an angel from heaven."

Pictures of Berliners watching support planes flying near Tempelhof

It seemed at first that the Allies could never reach the magic number of 4,000 tons a day; in fact, during the first few weeks they barely made a quarter of that, finally reaching the 1,000 ton mark by the end of the first month. Then, in July, the Air Force assigned General Tunner to oversee operations, and he had a careful plan that involved using each of the three air corridors as a one way street. Two would be used to fly the heavily laden, slower planes in while one would be used by the then emptied, faster planes. Soon, he had planes flying five deep and landing every three minutes, and once on the ground, each plane was unloaded within 30 minutes. A pilot had to remain with his plane while it was being unloaded, but he was treated to refreshments to keep him going during his long day.

A picture of the air corridors used in Berlin

By the end of July, the Americans were delivering 4,500 tons of supplies a day, and needless to say, the Soviets were not happy with the progress being made by the West. Naturally, they did nothing to support the relief efforts. On July 8, 1948, an *Associated Press* article reported, "The Russia authorities have disclaimed all responsibility for the safety of American aircraft supplying Berlin, it was officially revealed here today with the publication of an exchange of letters between the American and Russian control elements at the Berlin Air Safety Centre. The Russian notification came after the American controller had informed the other three Allies of a modification in the procedure of handling American flight information. The American controller said that the progress of American flights would in future be posted on a visual flight progress board, 'For the information of all other elements.'"

The article went on to report the Allies' successes, seemingly taunting the Soviets: "Despite bad weather which forced them to fly by instruments, U.S. pilots brought in more than 1,000 tons of supplies for Soviet-blockaded Berlin during the past 24 hours. Allied authorities have estimated that 2,000 tons of food a day are needed for the Western sectors, and the American planned to fly at least half of it. The British have kept their daily hauls secret for "security reasons." However, an idea of the size of their cargoes can be formed by the number of R.A.F. flights. Today British transports came in 209 times, compared with the 108 flights with which the Americans beat the 1,000 ton record."

Though the airlift continued to make progress during its first few months of operation, there were a number of problems along the way. Draper, Jr. explained, "After about two or three months we almost ran out of food. We had about ninety days' supply of coal, and about thirty days' supply of food when this started. We should have stocked up more before. We really didn't visualize that this blockade was going to happen. We should have taken action earlier and stocked food, but we hadn't, at least not very much. We had about thirty days' of food and some 90 days of coal. So we didn't have to worry about the coal right away. This started in early July. I would guess that it was about the end of August, when we were really running downhill. We weren't keeping even. We got down to three or four or five days' stock of food. So we had to face a strategic decision in Washington. There was one way we could save this situation if we were willing to take the risk, and that was to take all the DC-4s that we had around the world, Army planes and private airline planes, and substitute them for the DC-3s. The DC-4 will carry ten tons where the DC-3 carries two and a half. But it meant stripping our Army in Japan, it meant stripping our Army in Europe, and the airlines in the United States, of the only really available and useful carriage for troops if we were going to war. It would have meant a very real difference whether we had those planes immediately available or had to find a way to get them together again."

Desperate times call for desperate measures, and the Allies were pretty desperate, as were the German people. As such, according to Draper, Jr., "the decision was finally made to substitute, and we quietly stripped everywhere of these planes, and took them away from the airlines and the Army and sent them to Europe, substituted them, and put the DC-3s back in their place."

The results soon showed that everyone had made the right decision. Draper, Jr. concluded, "So immediately the level of food shipments by air went up. And by that time, the coal was also running out, and so some of these were then made coal wagons, the most expensive coal wagons the world ever saw. We tried dropping the coal in chutes, or as it was into big nets, or on the ground. By the time it got near the ground it was powder and blew away and it didn't work at all, so we had to land the planes and unload them just like the food. I rode one of those coal wagons one day from Berlin to Frankfurt and it was quite an experience. But it began to work.

Everything worked fine. The stocks were built up, the stockpiles of both food and coal."

Pictures of supply planes at Frankfurt

Chapter 5: More Than Just An Airlift

"If the Berlin Airlift was to be successful — and I never had any doubts but that it would be, then it would be more than just an airlift. It would be a propaganda weapon held up before the whole world. We should not hide it. And finally, knowing my men, I wanted to be able to give them the exact tonnage figures of each squadron to inspire them to do better. Why, this was one of my tools. Total tonnage figures for the past twenty-four-hour period came out at noon each day. These figures would be rushed into print and the paper sent on its way. Distribution was easy; all planes went into Berlin, and all planes returned to their bases. The papers were put on the first available plane out of Wiesbaden base, and picked up in Berlin by the first planes leaving for the other bases. The chief topic of conversation on every base was the daily tonnage records. Visitors to the Airlift were amazed by the spirit of competition. ... We encouraged enthusiasm with prizes — usually cigarettes, worth their weight in gold — for outstanding performances." – William H. Tunner

A picture of planes at Wiesbaden

Unwilling to shoot planes down from the skies, the Russians attempted to turn the airlift into a propaganda battle, telling people in one broadcast, "Haven't we heard that before? Think back. How was it again? Once upon a time our benefactors came with bombs and phosphor." For their part, the British wasted no time responding, reminding the Germans, "No longer night, and not yet day. And as the sun rises, bombers are readied. Bombers, once the heralds of death, today, in the summer 1948, in the service of Life and Freedom."

Meanwhile, the Americans had their own tools, most notably the Radio in the American Sector (RIAS) broadcasts. As William Heimlich, the head of U.S. intelligence in Berlin, explained, "RIAS did two things. It sustained the morale of people, not only of West Berlin, but of all Germany: it guaranteed to them finally that the Americans were there to stay; the Western Allies were there to stay; that there was now a firm wall between them and the…terror and the disaster of Soviet domination of their country. That was number one. Number two, I think that it was important for the Americans, particularly, to have a morale builder that they were finally standing up to the Soviet assaults and attacks. Everybody was so aware of those assaults in the press, in the Kommandantur, and the insults of not having any kind of personal contact with the Soviet Union, or its representative. The Americans particularly resented this. The British were much more philosophical about, and I expect due to their political sophistication. The Americans were not that sophisticated: we liked people to like us and we were finally convinced that the Soviets were not going to like us, we come to like the Germans better than we did the Soviets, although we had just finished fighting them, and we liked the idea of taking up at least verbal arms in their defense."

While the situation in the air was getting better, things on the ground were deteriorating. On September 6, 1948, Communists took over the Berlin Council House in order to prevent elections from taking place, and a few days later, America responded by using RIAS to incite protests against this move. At a gathering of more than 500,000 of the city's residents, held near the famed Brandenburg Gate, Reuter pleaded for continued help: "You peoples of the world. You people of America, of England, of France, look on this city, and recognize that this city, this people must not be abandoned -- cannot be abandoned!" Excited, the crowd pressed forward, crossing over into the Eastern sector and ripping down the Soviet flag. The soldiers on the ground responded by firing on the crowd, killing one young man.

What the Soviets failed to see was that they were losing an important demographic, namely the children who would soon grow into adults who could fight and vote. The West's air crews, however, seemed to know instinctively how to win over young hearts and minds. Halvorsen later recalled that, when the boys gathered to watch the planes land, "I wiggled the wings of the airplane, and they went crazy. I can still see their arms and hands up to the sky … Before I got donations from big candy companies, the children of America were sending me donations, and sending me money so we could go to the base exchange and buy the things to drop to the children of Berlin."

Picture of an American plane dropping candy in Berlin

The West's efforts led to a very interesting request from young Mercedes Wild who, as an adult, remembered writing a letter: "So I wrote to him: 'Dear Chocolate -- Uncle, you fly over Friedenau every day. Please drop a parachute over the garden with the white chickens. They've stopped laying. ... They think you're a chicken-hawk, and the eggs aren't coming any more, and their feathers are falling out. ... When you see the white chickens, drop it there. ... If you drop a parachute, I don't mind if you hit them. Your Mercedes."

Halvorsen was touched by Mercedes's concerns, and by the need for fresh eggs in a starving community. "I told my buddies who were dropping them. I said, 'When you're coming in to Tempelhof, drop on the approach, at apartment houses wherever you see them. We gotta hit Mercedes. We didn't hit Mercedes. Took a big pack of government candy in Berlin, mailed it to Mercedes." He included a note that read, "Dear Mercedes: If I did a couple of circuits over Friedenau, I'm sure I'd find the garden with the white chickens. But I'm afraid I haven't got the time. I hope that you will enjoy the enclosed. Your chocolate uncle, Gail Halvorsen."

That was all it took to make the girl a lifelong fan. "The chocolate was okay. But the important thing was the letter. He had written back. I had written to him, so I was waiting for an answer."

And I still have that letter. It was wonderful. My father had gone missing as a pilot during the war. Now I saw this Chocolate Uncle as my father who was showing me that he was there for me."

In time, the Berlin blockade and the airlift that followed came to be viewed as more of a fight for the minds and hearts of the Germans than it was to defeat the Communists there. On September 19, 1948, the *New York Times* offered an interesting insight: "The objective of the Russian blockade was fairly obvious. The Russians are evidently convinced that they cannot break the development of the Western German Government and the consolidation of Western Germany into the economy of the West. They are, therefore, seeking in every way possible to consolidate their own position in Eastern Europe and Eastern Germany. To this end they put the squeeze on Berlin. They cut-off supplies from one sector to another. They cut the electrical power. They even stopped the flow of medical supplies -- all on the pretext of "technical difficulties" on the main railway routes from Western Germany into the former capital. Their hope evidently was that within a short time the Germans would be forced by the shortages to take radical measures to break the blockade; that they would demand withdrawal of the Western powers and thus leave Berlin and the whole of Eastern Germany to the Soviet Union. The thirty-four-day supply of goods and the airlift defeated this strategy and the dramatic quality of the air operation has certainly heartened and emboldened the Berliner."

The author of the article, James Reston, further observed, "These Berliners are not the apathetic, gray-faced persons this reporter saw a year ago. They are probably not quite as reliable either, as many of the United States officials here think they are. But something has happened to them. They are certainly going through a process of reading of both sides of the question -- something new for this generation of Germans. All the evidence available suggests that their love of Marshal Vassily D. Sokolovsky, Soviet Military Governor, and the Russians is not unlimited. People living under a siege -- even former enemies -- are naturally drawn together, and hungry men naturally tend to support those who feed them against those who blockade their supplies. For the moment, therefore, the feeling between United States officials and the Germans is perhaps slightly on the dreamy side. Nevertheless the planes overhead night and day are a fairly strong argument in favor of the United States and for the moment the Berliner seems impressed. In the wider sphere of European politics too, United States officials feel the airlift has had a considerable effect. Berlin has become unfortunately, the symbol not of the German problem, but of the Russian problem and United States efforts here have undoubtedly been reassuring to the West. The feeling seems to be that the United States is keeping its word, and that is always refreshing thing, especially in these parts."

October brought continuous flights throughout the day and night, as well as increased concerns about how the Allies could possibly get enough fuel to the people of Berlin to keep them alive through the winter. No matter what happened, Clay was determined, and he told a reporter, "We are not going to be forced out of Berlin. We will increase [the air supply] and we can continue it indefinitely."

A picture of Germans collecting coal rations

On October 19, the *Star of India* enthusiastically reported, "Western Powers' delegates were to-day considering replies prepared by their experts to the Security Council's two questions on the Berlin dispute. Observers believed that the Council will, without further delay, pass a resolution condemning the Soviet blockade when it resumes consideration of the position tomorrow. Opinion in favour of such action hardened among the six 'neutral' members of the Council during the weekend, mainly as a result of the Soviet delegate M. Andrei Vyshinksy's refusal to answer the questions put by Dr. Juan Bramuglia, Acting Chairman of the Council. Dr. Bramuglia asked the Four Powers to (1) explain how the travel restrictions in Berlin and between the eastern and western zones of Germany arose, and (2) explain circumstantially the agreement involved in the instruments given to the Military Governors in Berlin and the reasons that prevent implementation of the agreement."

The governments hired 18,000 Berliners, more than 9,000 of them female, to build a new airport so that they could land more planes. Of course, the planes could not fly themselves, so men like Ken Slaker were soon called back into service. He had dropped bombs during the war and noted how different things were in peacetime: "We'd just been 20 minutes into Eastern Germany when we lost both engines simultaneously. And went through emergency procedures. We couldn't get them started again. So I just bailed out. I said to myself, this is it. When I got my memory back and it was daylight. And then I heard a noise. And there was the sound of an airlift aircraft overhead. So I knew where I was. Let's say that I was right on the route to Berlin. I realized I was in a real, real trouble. I ran face-to-face with a German. And I told him, where's Fulda. He said, 'Fulda nein good.' I said, Fulda's good for me. I told him I'm an American pilot on the airlift. And when I said that he had immediate respect for me. He opened his coat and pulled out some papers. And they were his discharge papers from the American prison for two years and so we were able to communicate."

That day, Rudolph Schnabel took the downed pilot into his own home, where, according to his wife Magdalena, "I made something to eat and said, 'Come on, you eat too.' At first he said: 'No, you haven't got enough.' So I said: What feeds two will also feed three.' He was a very good looking man, neat as a pin, tip-top, with the uniform and all ... Ken said goodbye very nicely and so did my husband and we hugged, and said: "Let's hope it'll be okay. And I said: 'Say a quick Our Father and it'll be all right.' And he said, 'You say one too. Then it will be all right.' Schnabel made contact with agents willing to help Slaker escape."

In what was taking the shape of a classic espionage movie, Slaker managed to learn which way he needed to go, although the information was not particularly encouraging. He continued, "They told us what we had to do to get through the border. That they'd buy -- and I gave them some West marks, they bought off the East German policeman who was on the bridge on the river from 8:00 to 8:30 when the Soviet guard changed. Well, my heart was in my mouth when we started crossing the bridge because that German policeman was coming straight towards us. And about two meters from us he stopped, turned around and ignored us. So he'd been paid off. ... And so we started up the incline. My back was killing me. I got halfway up the ridge. My back gave out and I fell and rolled back down to the bottom. And the girl said, "The captain has fallen." And they stopped. They came back down there and they pulled me up that incline. If they had not have done that, I would not be here." Though Schnabel was later captured by Communists and cruelly questioned, he never turned in his new friend, and Slaker was eventually able to return the favor by helping the couple who had saved his life make it to the West.

Chapter 6: Childish Stunts

"Later, after it was apparent that the Airlift was effective, the Russians resorted to many silly and childish stunts in their efforts to harass us. Their first action was to announce that on the morrow they would be flying in formation over Berlin and East Germany, including the corridors. I protested through channels, as well as to the Four-Power Air Safety Center in Berlin, but I was convinced all along that the Russians were bluffing. I put out orders to all pilots to continue boring ahead and not to pay any attention to the Russians if they did show up. The threatened formation never developed. … On occasion they staged anti-aircraft practice, with a plane towing a target for the guns below to shoot at. Sometimes the shells burst in the corridor. They were seen by the pilots and were sometimes close, but they were never more than a morale threat. On some occasions, as our planes lumbered up the corridor, a Russian jet would zoom out of nowhere towing a sleeve target, with another fighter zipping along pouring machine-gun bullets into it Sometimes Russian pilots buzzed us as we proceeded up the corridors." – William H. Tunner

The Berlin Airlift had been going full force for just five months when winter weather began to periodically ground the planes. Desperate for food and unsure when the next shipment would be arriving, some people gave into the Soviets' offers to provide them with food from Eastern Europe in exchange for their West Berlin ration cards. However, most of them remained dubious of the offer, which proclaimed, "Since 1 August every Berlin housewife -- in any sector -- can register her ration card in the Soviet sector. Supplies to Berlin's millions are guaranteed by the deliveries from the Soviet Union, Poland and Czechoslovakia."

To make already difficult matters worse, the airlift suffered another setback with its first major accident. On November 6, 1948, *Le Monde of Paris* reported, "The American occupation zone in Germany has been for its part the site of two accidents: at Gramisch, in Bavaria, a D.80 clipped itself on two houses. The pilot was killed, the houses burned. At Neubiberg, Captain Vincent Bracha had more luck: he successfully landed his Thunderbolt, which was completely destroyed, off the runway. The pilot was only slightly injured."

Undeterred, everyone remained determined to see the mission through, and a few days later the magazine carried another article that told readers, "Assuredly, the Americans do not intend to give the Russians the impression of ceding to the power of the blockade. The tendency in contrast is always firmness, as in the testimony of M. Foster Dulles at the United Nations, conforming to directives coming from Washington immediately following the election of M. Truman. But any significant changes in western Germany will have to wait until after the reshuffling of the cabinet and the inauguration ceremony of next January 20."

As the year wound down to an end, Berliners also began to plan for their December 5 election of new city officials. Again, the Soviets did all that they could to intimidate people into voting for their candidates, and when they realized they would not get their way, they ignored the open elections altogether and appointed Friedrich Ebert as mayor of their part of the city. Meanwhile, Reuter was returned to office in the West.

Ebert

Eventually, he weather in Germany began to adversely affect the airlift. Draper, Jr. explained, "[I]n November we had an early winter, and early fog; the fog's bad in Berlin, anyway; but this year it was worse than they had ever seen, I guess, and it came down about the first of November and it just stuck. It meant that you had to go…on instruments entirely. In the meantime, the Russians were buzzing the planes. They didn't shoot any down, but they came right near us. It's a wonder there weren't any accidents, and so starting a war, because that would have probably done it. Anyway, this fog came down and it meant that you had to land every five or six or ten minutes instead of every two, and the stockpiles ran down again. It ran right through December and by the third or fourth or fifth of January we were down to two days again. And it looked like curtains. If that fog had stayed another three weeks we probably would have had to run up the white flag. We probably couldn't have gone on. You can't have people starving, and keep on with the occupation. But the weather lifted about the fifth of January, it was fine, and immediately we restored the situation."

Despite the adverse conditions, December brought the Christmas holiday, and people in America remained enthusiastic about helping the less fortunate in Europe. On December 26, the *St. Louis Post-Dispatch* reminded its readers, "Alben Barkley, United States Vice-President-elect, declared today 'it would be unthinkable that we pull out of Berlin. Our people are determined to continue the air lift.' Addressing a press conference on his Berlin stop of a

European trip, Barkley said there is 'no question that the United States Congress will favor continuing the air lift to Berlin.' Air Secretary Stuart Symington, another United States notable here for the holidays, told reporters at the same conference that there is no reason why air lift tonnage 'cannot go to whatever figure is necessary.' He said more planes are being purchase for the air lift task force."

Barkley

As 1949 approached, the RIAS found a new way to encourage those suffering from cold and hunger. Berlin resident Hans-Günther Richardi remembered, "My mother suffered greatly from her husband's absence, and of course it was vital for her to have a source of information to tell her how he was. And every night on RIAS, about half past nine after the news -- there came: Task Force against Inhumanity. And they passed on news from the different camps. And one evening, when I was eight, my mother was washing me in the bathtub. I'll never forget it. She was listening to the radio and the Task Force against Inhumanity came on and the voice said: 'Railway engineer Günther Richardi has died in the Neubrandenburg Concentration Camp.' My mother had no idea it was coming. She let out a single cry. It was a disaster for her."

At the same time, the Soviets became very adept at utilizing the hurt felt by families who were far from their loved ones. Tunner explained, "Of all Communist hostile acts, perhaps the most damaging was the poison-pen campaign. Mysterious letters would come to our pilots, letters mailed both in Germany and in the United States, reporting the infidelity of wives or sweethearts. Some degree of bitterness already existed between many couples over the extended periods of temporary duty, and even to those husbands who normally shared a firm mutual trust with their wives the letters could cause nagging doubts and a resulting drop in morale."

Chapter 7: Broke the Back of the Berlin Blockade

"I thought of the people of Berlin, still getting by on short rations, often getting up in the middle of the night to cook if that was when the four hours of electricity a day was allotted them, and what this extra coal would mean to them. All over Berlin, I knew, the people knew something big was going on. Those big planes, thundering in at a quicker beat than ever before, without cessation for twenty-four hours, would be the subject of every conversation in Berlin that Sunday. My skin prickled with pride at the role my men had played in this great demonstration of generous power on the part of our free nations. It was that day, that Easter Sunday, I'm sure, that broke the back of the Berlin blockade. From then on we never fell below one thousand tons a day; the land blockade was pointless. A month later, May 21, 1949, the Soviets grudgingly reached the same conclusion and ended it. Surface traffic began to move. " – William H. Tunner

For all that the West made much of their humanitarian efforts to save the German people from starvation, there was another angle on the Berlin crisis, one that received less press and was certainly made less of by the American government. This was, of course, the Allies' counter blockade that aimed to prevent the shipment of Western goods into East Berlin. On January 16, 1949, the *New York Times* reported, "Safely over the worst flying weather, pilots of the Berlin airlift are daily strengthening the conviction among Germans as well as Western Allied occupation forces that they have clinched their point -- that the blockade of Berlin has failed. This conviction also appears to be spreading even into the Soviet sector and zone. Western Berliners circulate reports tending to support the view that the economic pinch is becoming increasingly more evident in the East than in the West. They noted that the Max-Huette factory, a large steel plant in the Soviet zone recently requested contributions of shovels and other tools, formerly obtained from Western Germany to aid in continued operation and production. A brown coal plant in Hoyerswerda in the Soviet zone published its need for sixty-nine tons of rolled steel sheets, indispensable for the continued production of coal briquettes. Soviet officials themselves have been prompt on occasions when they encountered representatives of the Western powers to denounce the counter-blockade as 'unfair' and restrictive. They have complained bitterly about conditions that have necessitated the closing down of various industries in their territory, while proclaiming stoutly that no actual blockade of Berlin existed."

Moreover, there was soon a much more important factor introduced to the airlift, one which would prove to be the turning point in many people's lives. The British government authorized its pilots to use the planes returning from dropping their supplies to fly people wanting to leave Berlin out of the city. One of those who got away from the city was a 10 year old named Peter Zimmerman, who recalled decades later how his flight ended in disaster: "There were hours of waiting. They kept saying the plane wasn't ready or it had to be repaired. I don't think we were afraid, at least, I wasn't, and my sister didn't really know what was happening. … There was a slight scraping sound and a moment later there was a louder scraping sound, and then another. … All I can remember is that last loud bang, and then the fuel exploding. You can't imagine how bad it was -- utter chaos, utter helplessness. Pieces of the plane were lying around. The plane was on fire. There was a terrible smell, and the most terrible thing of all was a smell of grilled meat. It was roasted human flesh."

Zimmerman soon learned that both his mother and sister had been killed in the crash. John Eddy, the pilot that day, later explained what went wrong: "Coming back from Berlin as far as the flight was concerned, the take off and everything was normal. There was no, no ... it wasn't until we got towards Lübeck itself that they told us that there was this full cloud cover and, and how far it was from the ground, from the airfield surface. And they said, well, the instruction was to descend and do a visual circuit. And when we broke cloud it was inky black. There was not a sign of a light or anything. But unfortunately the trees stretched up to 200, 300 feet. And we hit them. And as far as I know, I pushed the throttles forward but we didn't get away. And the next thing I knew I was lying on my back on the ground, looking up at the sky and seeing all the stars, which was ridiculous because it was full cloud cover. But I could see every star in the sky."

While there were some accidents during the airlift, the planes used to carry people and supplies were manned by some of the best pilots the West had to offer, and they rarely crashed. That said, maintaining them became an increasing burden, and Air Force mechanics had a difficult job keeping the heavily used planes in the air. Furthermore, there were not enough mechanics available to do the job.

Tunner had a solution, but it was not a very popular one at first. "When I arrived in Germany, the hard-and-fast regulations against fraternization made it difficult to use Germans except in the most menial capacity. As our maintenance problems multiplied, however, we began to consider more and more seriously the possibility of using German mechanics. These problems were serious to begin with, but as our increased efficiency brought about a higher utilization rate of planes, additional maintenance was required. … All our units were under strength. In addition, the shortage of adequate equipment, from heavy cranes on down to such basic items as screw drivers, curtailed the work output per man. The idea of augmenting our maintenance forces with

German mechanics followed naturally. For years the world had heard about the great Luftwaffe; surely the German Air Force had had mechanics. Now we needed them to help us help the fellow citizens in Berlin. The first stumbling block was the non-fraternization regulation; we could knock ourselves out feeding the Germans, but we couldn't see them socially or employ them in any but menial capacities. Permission to use Germans as aircraft technicians could come only from General Clay himself. ... I told him...there weren't enough good maintenance men to go around. 'But I think I can whip it,' I said, 'if you will allow me to hire some skilled German mechanics.' 'Go ahead and do it,' he said."

Once he had permission to hire the German mechanics, Tunner still had to find some, and on this point he put his years of experience to good use by figuring out an effective way to locate just the men he needed. "I suggested they find a former German Air Force maintenance officer who would, in turn, be able to locate mechanics for us. ... I told him what I wanted, and he delivered. Almost overnight excellent German mechanics began flowing in. Now we had only two problems to overcome: the language barrier, and the unfamiliarity on the part of the Germans with our big C-54's. [The German officer] organized a translation section to put our training manuals into German as the first step in an extensive training program. In the meantime, we assigned maintenance personnel who could speak German to serve as supervisors. As German civilians acquired experience, those who could speak English were able to step into key positions, thus reducing the load on the German-speaking maintenance officers. The German mechanics proved to be so capable that eventually eighty- five of them were assigned to each squadron. We had more German mechanics than American!"

A picture of a C-54 during the Berlin Airlift

By the time the winter of 1949 began to come to its blustery end, the world was ready to see some sort of peaceful resolution to the situation in Berlin. Indeed, even the media did its part to push for some sort of mutually acceptable end to the blockade; on February 3, Kingsbury Smith, a correspondent with the *International News Service*, sent a wire to Stalin himself, asking the Soviet dictator, "If the Governments of the United States of America, the United Kingdom, and France agreed to postpone the establishment of a separate Western German State, pending a meeting of the Council of Foreign Ministers to consider the German problem as a whole, would the Government of the USSR be prepared to remove the restrictions which the Soviet authorities have posed on communications between Berlin and Western zones of Germany?" Stalin sent back a positive reply: "Provided the United States of America, Great Britain, and France observed the conditions set forth in the third question, the Soviet Government sees no obstacle to lifting transport restrictions, on the understanding, however, that transport and trade restrictions introduced by the Three Powers should be lifted simultaneously."

By February 14, 1949, the *Times of London* informed readers of political maneuverings in Europe that might help bring about some resolution: "Professor Ernst Reuter, the chief burgomaster, announced to-day that Mr. Bevin, the British Foreign Secretary, intends to visit

Berlin. He said he hoped that the visit would take place in the next few months if Mr. Bevin's health permits, and added that Berliners would make him welcome. Reporting to the City Assembly on his visits last week to London and Paris, Herr Reuter said that the Lord Mayor of London had expressed his sympathy for Berlin in its difficult position, and his admiration for the behaviour of its citizens. He had invited the Lord Mayor to visit Berlin. Herr Reuter emphasized that both in London and in Paris there had been discussions only, not negotiations, but, he said, the fact that even discussions were possible signified a great improvement in the atmosphere. In London he had been sympathetically received, and had found complete agreement on the most important issues affecting Berlin. He had left with the conviction that all the inevitable barriers had been broken. On currency, the "most urgent problem," he was convinced that the existence of two currencies in western Berlin -- the west mark and the east mark, which have circulated simultaneously since the introduction of currency reform last summer -- was coming to an end, although he was not authorized to mention any date. This change would mean that a whole series of problems in the western sectors would solve themselves."

While all sides may have wished to bring about an end to the blockade, no one was willing to make the first move and lose face. In hindsight, it seems that the Soviet Union might have been hoping that the Western powers would tire of the stress and expense of maintaining the airlift and give up, but that was constantly being proven wrong. In the spring of 1949, the *New York Times* reported that the planes were shipping more food and fuel than ever before: "All airlift records were broken today when American and British airmen flew 8,246.1 short tons of food and coal into Berlin on 922 flights in the twenty-four hours ending at noon. The record was established on the 290th day of the airlift. It eclipsed the previous high set Feb. 25-26 when 8,025.8 tons were brought to the blockaded city. Since the start of airlift 1,327,226.4 short tons have been flown into the city on 166,984 flights."

This new record proved to be the breaking point for the Soviets, who soon negotiated an agreement to lift the blockade on May 12, 1949. One excited reporter wrote, "The hottest spot in the Cold War is eliminated. Allied vehicles await the removal of the barriers and the signal for the dash to Berlin. With the opening of the gates a new chapter in postwar history begins to unroll down German highways. Just 10 months and 23 days after the capital was sealed off from the ground, traffic is rolling toward Europe's number one trouble spot. It's a day of [joy] for [the] band of men in the airlift who kept Berliners eating while they were held in an iron ring."

Likewise, the *Sydney Morning Herald* out of Australia reported, "Berlin people really knew the blockade was off when at one minute past midnight last night -- the big Soviet-controlled Klingenberg power station switched on the lights in the Western sectors of the city; and Soviet-controlled Berlin radio announced: "At this moment, all traffic and trade restrictions between the Soviet zone of Germany and the Western zone and within Berlin imposed since January 1, 1948, are being lifted on the orders of the four occupation Powers." Berlin is the happiest city in the world to-day. After months of tension and austerity and the recent days when skepticism tempered the hopes of more than two million people besieged in the Western sectors, the whole city is lit with jubilation to-day. Great crowds -- singing, laughing, and cheering every Allied vehicle -- are parading the ruin-lined streets decorating tramcars with bunting garlands and slogans -- "Berlin lives again," and "hail to the new era." With trains, lorries and a never-ending stream of airlift planes pouring supplies into the city's larder, West Berlin is tasting normal life for the first time for 11 months."

Indeed, there was dancing in the streets and all sorts of celebrations as the first resources transported by ground made their way into the city. Richardi described the scene: "And now trucks were coming in from the West -- and interestingly, the first thing they brought was masses of oranges. And I said to my friend, 'let's go down to the end of the Autobahn where they arrive and maybe we'll be lucky.' And they were throwing oranges to the crowd -- still nicely wrapped back then -- and some kids were lucky and they caught some. But I didn't get any, and neither did my friend, and we went home really downhearted. Just like kids are, because they would have been my very first oranges. So I came home, went into the kitchen and I couldn't believe my eyes. There on the table were two oranges, cut open like a water lily."

When Clay was asked for his reaction to the good news, he took the opportunity to praise the people he and his men had been honored to serve: "The end of the blockade does not merely mean that trains and trucks are moving again. It has a deeper significance. The people of Berlin have earned their right to freedom and to be accepted by those who love freedom everywhere. The people of Berlin, ranked with the American and British pilots who fed the city as the real heroes of the blockade."

Officially, the Berlin Airlift did not end until September 30, 1949, mainly because the Allies wanted to make sure that there would not be any excessive shortages in Berlin. The following month, the city itself was divided in two, with East Berlin remaining in the hands of the Soviets while West Berlin, with the help of the Allies, soon became an independent city again.

According to Tunner, "The Berlin airlift was the first great challenge — and the first great humanitarian airlift — that the United States Air Force met as an independent service. That a prodigious airlift effort accompanied this blockade is evidenced by the following impressive statistics:

1,783,572.7 tons of supplies delivered,

62,749 passengers flown,

189,963 total flights,

586,827 total flying hours, and

92,061,862 aircraft miles flown by C-47 and C-54 transports.

Sadly, this came at the cost of 31 American fatalities during Berlin airlift operations, 28 of which were Air Force personnel."

The Berlin blockade was one of the first major confrontations of the Cold War, but it would hardly be the last. In fact, in some ways it was merely the start of a protracted contest over Berlin, one that would continue until the fall of the Berlin Wall in 1989.

Online Resources

Other Cold War titles by Charles River Editors

Other 20th century history titles by Charles River Editors

Other titles about the Berlin Airlift on Amazon

Bibliography

Beschloss, Michael R. (2003), The Conquerors: Roosevelt, Truman and the Destruction of Hitler's Germany, 1941–1945, Simon and Schuster, ISBN 0-7432-6085-6

Canwell, Diane (2008), Berlin Airlift, the, Gretna: Pelican Publishing, ISBN 978-1-58980-550-7

Cherny, Andrei (2008), The Candy Bombers: The Untold Story of the Berlin Airlift and America's Finest Hour, New York: G.P. Putnam's Sons, ISBN 978-0-399-15496-6

Eglin, Roger; Ritchie, Berry (1980), Fly me, I'm Freddie, London, UK: Weidenfeld and Nicolson, ISBN 0-297-77746-7

Gaddis, John Lewis. *The Cold War: A New History*. New York: Penguin Press, 2005.

Gere, Edwin. The Unheralded: Men and Women of the Berlin Blockade and Airlift. Victoria, B.C.: Trafford Publishing, Inc., 2006.

Harrington, Daniel F. Berlin on the Brink: The Blockade, the Airlift, and the Early Cold War (2012), University of Kentucky Press, Lexington, KY, ISBN 978-08131-3613-4.

Jackson, Robert. The Berlin Airlift. Wellingborough, Northhamptonshire, England: Stephens, 1988.

Large, David Clay. *Berlin* (New York: Basic Books, 2000), 522.https://www.questia.com/read/100504423.

Larson, Deborah Welch. "The Origins of Commitment: Truman and West Berlin," Journal of Cold War Studies, 13#1 Winter 2011, pp. 180–212

Lewkowicz, N (2008), The German Question and the Origins of the Cold War, Milan: IPOC, ISBN 978-88-95145-27-3

Miller, Roger Gene (2000), To Save a City: The Berlin Airlift, 1948–1949, Texas A&M University Press, ISBN 0-89096-967-1

Parrish, Thomas. Berlin in the Balance: The Blockade, the Airlift, the First Major Battle of the Cold War. Reading, Massachusetts: Addison-Wesley, 1998.

Pearcy, Arthur. Berlin Airlift. Shrewsbury, England: Airlife Publishing, 1997.

Schrader, Helena P. The Blockade Breakers: The Berlin Airlift (2011)

Stent, Angela (2000), Russia and Germany Reborn: Unification, the Soviet Collapse, and the New Europe, Princeton University Press, ISBN 978-0-691-05040-9

Stern, Fritz. *Five Germanys I Have Known*. New York: Farrar, Straus, and Giroux, 2006.

Tunner, LTG (USAF) William H. (1998) [1964], Over the Hump, Duell, Sloan and Pearce (USAF History and Museums Program)

Turner, Henry Ashby (1987), The Two Germanies Since 1945: East and West, Yale University Press, ISBN 0-300-03865-8

Tusa, Ann and John Tusa. The Berlin Airlift. New York: Atheneum, 1988.

Zubok, Vladislav M. A Failed Empire: The Soviet Union in the Cold War from Stalin to Gorbachev (Chapel Hill, NC: University of North Carolina Press, 2007).

Wettig, Gerhard (2008), Stalin and the Cold War in Europe, Rowman & Littlefield, ISBN 0-7425-5542-9

Made in the USA
Middletown, DE
28 November 2017